# Word  Bird's ™

# Happy Birthday, Word Bird!

Published in the United States of America by The Child's World®, Inc.
PO Box 326
Chanhassen, MN 55317-0326
800-599-READ
**www.childsworld.com**

**Project Manager** Mary Berendes
**Editor** Katherine Stevenson, Ph.D.
**Designer** Ian Butterworth

**Library of Congress Cataloging-in-Publication Data**
Moncure, Jane Belk.
Happy birthday, Word Bird! / by Jane Belk Moncure.
p. cm.
Summary: Word Bird reviews the months of the year
as he tries to figure out when his birthday will be.
ISBN 1-56766-989-1 (lib. : alk. paper)
[1. Months—Fiction. 2. Birds—Fiction.]    I. Title.
PZ7.M739 Hap 2002
[E]—dc21
2001006037

# Word Bird's

# Happy Birthday, Word Bird!

by Jane Belk Moncure
*illustrated by* Chris McEwan

"Is my birthday in January?" asked Word Bird.

"No," said Mama Bird.

"January is the time
for snow

and snowballs
and snowpeople."

"Is my birthday
in February?"

"No," said Mama.
"February is the time for

valentines

and candy hearts."

"Is my birthday in March?"

"No," said Papa Bird.
"March is the time for

shamrocks

and baseball

and kites."

"Is my birthday in April?"

"No," said Mama.
"April is the time for

showers

and bunnies

and eggs."

"Is my birthday in May?"

"No," said Mama.
"May is the time for

flowers

and
Mother's Day."

"Is my birthday in June?"

"No," said Papa.
"June is the time for

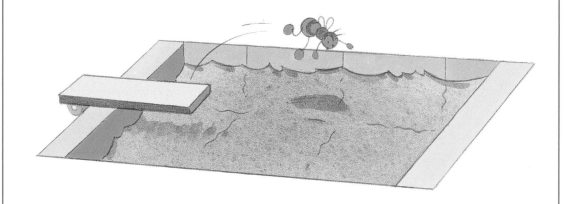

swimming pools

and Father's Day."

"Is my birthday in July?"

"No," said Papa.
"July is the time for

parades

and fireworks."

"Is my birthday in August?"

"No," said Mama.
"August is the time for

picnics

and fishing."

"Is my birthday
in September?"

"No," said Papa. "September is the time for books,

pencils,

crayons,

and a lunchbox."

"Is my birthday
in October?"

"No," said Mama.
"October is the time for

jack o'-lanterns

and Halloween ghosts."

"Is my birthday
in November?"

"No," said Papa.
"November is the time for

football

and cider."

"Is my birthday
in December?"

Can you guess what
Mama and Papa said?

# "Surprise!"

"Happy birthday,
Word Bird!"

# Can you read these words with Word Bird?

January

July

February

August

March

September

April

October

May

November

June

December